This library edition published in 2015 by Walter Foster Jr.,
a division of Quarto Publishing Group USA Inc.
3 Wrigley, Suite A
Irvine, CA 92618

Distributed in the United States and Canada by
Lerner Publisher Services
241 First Avenue North
Minneapolis, MN 55401 U.S.A.
www.lernerbooks.com

First Library Edition

Library of Congress Cataloging-in-Publication Data

Razo, Rebecca J.
  The monsters under my bed / Story by Rebecca J. Razo ; Illustrations by Diana Fisher. --
Library edition.
      pages cm. -- (Watch me draw)
ISBN 978-1-93958-137-2
1. Monsters in art--Juvenile literature. 2. Bedtime--Juvenile literature. 3. Drawing--
Technique--Juvenile literature. I. Fisher, Diana (Diana L.), illustrator. II. Title.
  NC825.M6R39 2015
  743'.87--dc23
                                                                2013011684

012015
18582

9 8 7 6 5 4 3 2 1

The Monsters Under My Bed

Story by Rebecca J. Razo • Illustrations by Diana Fisher

"Come, little one," my mommy said.
"It's very late and time for bed."

"But I can't go to sleep!" I said with a pout.
"As soon as you leave, the monsters come out."

Draw the alarm clock!

"Really?" Mom said, her eyes open wide.
"Who are these monsters? Where do they hide?"

"One is purple and orange. His name is Fred.
And most of the time, he stays under my bed."

Draw Fred!

"But where is Fred now?" Mom asked with a grin. "He's not under the bed—"

"Because he's in my toy bin!"

GO MONSTERS!

Draw the lion!

"I see," Mom said, her voice full of surprise.
"Does Fred also have big, googly eyes?"

"Why, no," I said. "You must have seen Gail.
She's got green, googly eyes and a long, curly tail."

Draw Gail!

"Gail and Fred sound like an interesting pair.
Do any more monsters give you a scare?"

"Well, there's Harry and Daisy and Esther and
Moe. And Claude wears black sneakers with
shoelaces that glow."

Draw Claude!

"Seven monsters!" Mom said. "That must be a sight. Why do you think they only come out at night?"

"They only come out when I can't fall sleep. Then they slink and they squeak, and they crawl and they creep. They make lots of noises that frighten me so. And one time a monster even bid me 'Hello!'"

Draw Harry!

"And what do you do when these monsters come out?
Do you jump out of bed? Do you scream? Do you shout?"

"I'm too frightened to look, so I stay tucked in bed,
with my eyes closed tight and blankets over my head."

Draw Daisy!

"My sweet little one. You've got nothing to fear. There's nothing so scary about those noises you hear. There aren't any monsters hiding under your bed, and there's no purple monster whose name is called Fred. There aren't monsters outside or out in the hall. In fact, there are not any monsters at all."

GO MONSTERS!

Draw Esther!

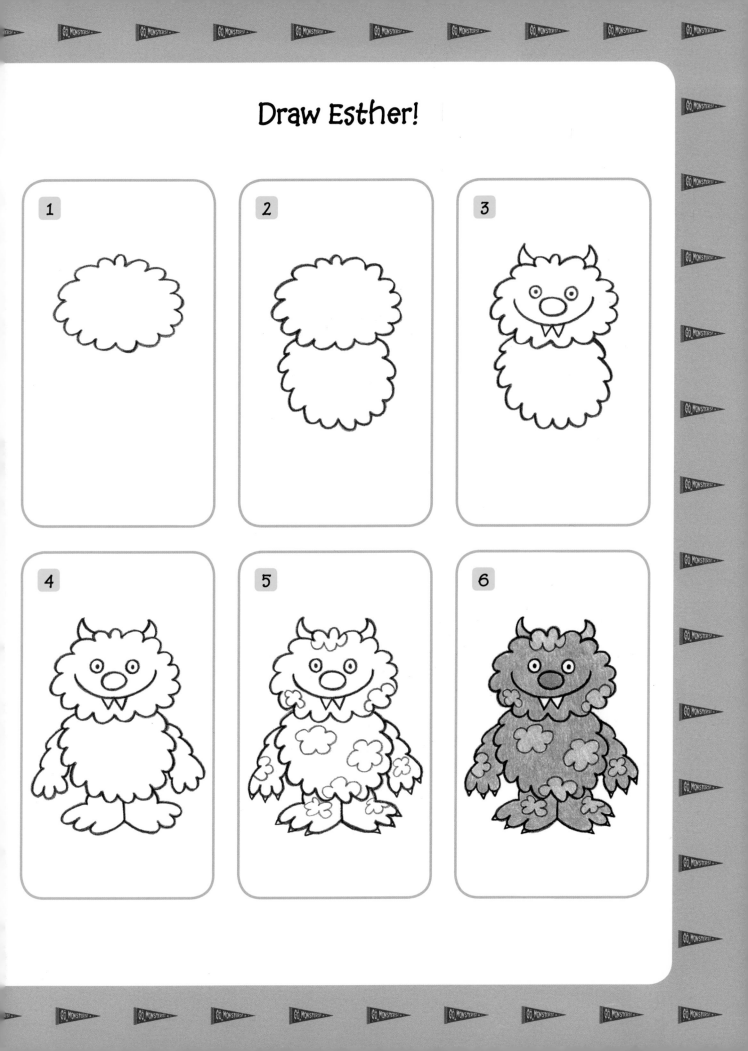

"Then what are those noises?" I said with a frown.

"What you hear late at night is the house settling down. When a house goes to sleep, it sometimes makes sounds. It squeaks and it creaks, and it hums all around. It's perfectly normal for a house to do this. Now do you believe that no monsters exist?"

Draw the House!

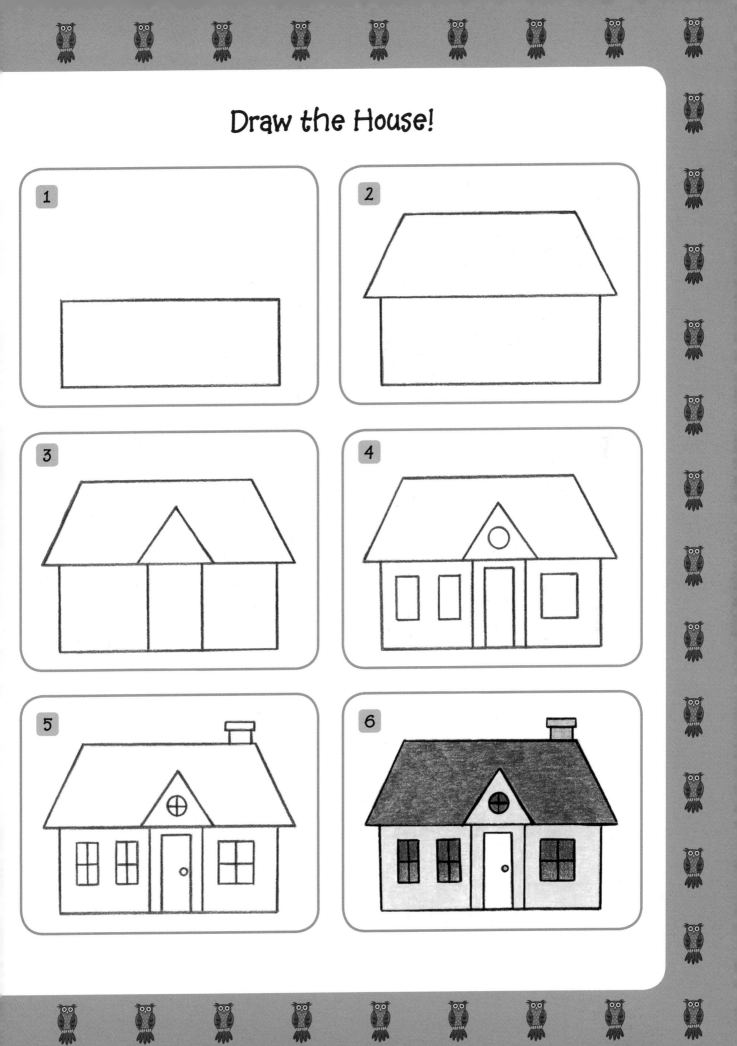

I thought for a moment and looked under my bed. Did I only *imagine* a monster named Fred? Then I suddenly realized that I had been wrong, and those monsters were pretend friends I'd had all along!

Draw Moe!

I had created the furry gang in my head, and I thought of them often at night in my bed. And while the house settled in with its squeaks and its creaks, it was thinking of them that helped get me to sleep! Fred's a bit silly; Gail likes to smile; Harry, Daisy, and Moe have a great sense of style; Esther is cuddly, and Claude is quite tall. Now I wonder why I ever felt scared at all!

Draw the teddy bear!

The end.